PRIMARY TOPICS
LIGHT

A Resource Book for Teachers
DOROTHY J. TAYLOR
DAVID CRISPIN

CONTENTS		Page
INTRODUCTION	....	2
TOPIC ONE	OCCASIONS FOR CANDLES	3
TOPIC TWO	GLORIOUS GLASS	9
TOPIC THREE	LIGHT	15
TOPIC FOUR	THREE DAYS IN THE CHRISTIAN CALENDAR ..	21
TOPIC FIVE	HANUKKAH	27

BFSS
National RE Centre

INTRODUCTION

Authors:
Dorothy J. Taylor is a lecturer and former Advisory Teacher (Primary RE)
David Crispin BA is the Primary Adviser to the BFSS National RE Centre at the West London Institute of Higher Education.

Acknowledgements
The authors wish to thank all those who supported them in, and contributed to the production of this book. We would particularly like to mention Ken Oldfield, Simon Potter, Jane Bevans, Christine Rendle, Terry Tiernan and Paul Crowe. Special thanks to G. M. Barham, the Head Teacher of St. Andrew's and St. Mark's School, Surbiton, and Canon J. C. Blair-Fish, previous Vicar of St. Mark's Church, Surbiton.
Front cover photograph by Simon Potter.
Back cover photograph and illustrations by David Crispin.
Illustration on page 15 by Terry Tiernan.

Series: Primary Topics

ISBN 1 872012 02 7

Copies of this booklet can be obtained from:
Simon Potter (Resources Officer)
BFSS National RE Centre
West London Institute of Higher Education
Lancaster House, Borough Road, Isleworth,
Middlesex TW7 5DU
Telephone: 01-568 8741 Ext. 2658

We cheer ourselves in the darkening months of the year by planning work associated with those festivals of light which have meaning for particular groups of children in our school. For children of Christian families the season of Advent, with its wreath of evergreens and candles, may be a significant festival of light. For children of Hindu background Diwali may be the highlight of the season. Christmas has meaning for many, both as a cultural festival of lights and as a celebration of the birth of the child whom Christians describe as their Light and Sun.

Some teachers will introduce a particular festival of light as a starting point for learning about its celebration locally and in other countries and for listening to stories which are associated with that festival. Other teachers may introduce a general topic associated with LIGHT, through which children may develop concepts, to enrich their understanding of the meaning of the religious celebrations introduced at a later stage of the project work or on some subsequent occasion. Both types of introduction are valid and are represented in the following pages.

Growing confidence in using material from many religious traditions and cultures in formulating programmes of religious education enables us to become more aware of the need to identify the commonly held objectives described in agreed syllabuses, so that we can justify our claims that such programmes are balanced and devised to meet the needs of our pupils. Diagrams in this booklet make four points in this respect. One or two are intended to remind us of the cross-curricular opportunities of basic interest topics. Several draw attention, through shaded boxes on the diagrams, to the implicit and explicit objectives for R.E. found in Primary sections of many agreed syllabuses. Some indicate, through similar boxes, concepts which are related to religious ideas, as a hint that our enthusiasm for developing skills, extending knowledge and providing creative opportunities should be matched by our analysis of the less tangible potential of the topic. All are reminders that, as teachers, we have the privilege of assessing the capabilities of children in our care and of making plans for R.E. which take account of those capacities, of local community groupings and contacts, and of our own expertise.

Designed and printed by BPCC Northern Printers Limited, Stanley Road, Blackpool

OCCASIONS FOR CANDLES

From early childhood candles have particular significance and excitement in the family circle. Toddlers have the help of their parents in blowing out their first birthday candles and this day represents a milestone for parents. Slightly older children welcome the idea of a nightlight in their bedroom, sensing the companionship of that light and the reassurance it seems to offer. Some children are taken to church to see the Paschal candle; others go into the synagogue and count the seven branches of the menorah. Thai children watch their candles, mounted in lotus shapes, float across the pond or downstream at Loi Kratong, as an offering to the river spirits who will help them get rid of misfortune.

To some people candles represent the idea of banishment of evil. The light in the carved pumpkin at Hallowe'en was once regarded as a means of keeping the farm and its animals safe from harm. To others candles represent the idea of welcome, the welcome given to Rama on his return from exile or that given to the infant Jesus each Christmas time. From Greek times candles have symbolised life and the birthday candle stresses that idea. For some, candles represent the soul at death and so memorial candles may be lit, the flickering light symbolising the journey of the soul towards heaven.

So, in family custom, in folk tradition and in religious observance candles, with their powerful symbolism, are commonplace.

MANY CANDLES

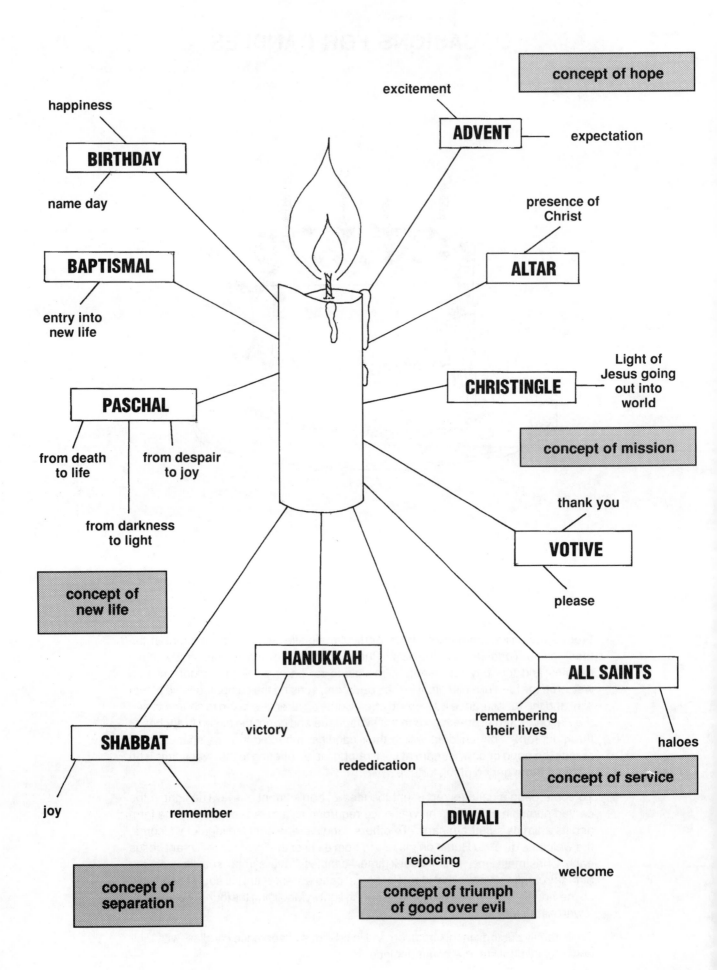

happiness

BIRTHDAY

name day

BAPTISMAL

entry into
new life

PASCHAL

from death
to life

from despair
to joy

from darkness
to light

concept of
new life

excitement

concept of hope

ADVENT

expectation

presence of
Christ

ALTAR

Light of
Jesus going
out into
world

CHRISTINGLE

concept of mission

thank you

VOTIVE

please

HANUKKAH

victory

rededication

SHABBAT

joy

remember

concept of
separation

ALL SAINTS

remembering
their lives

haloes

concept of service

DIWALI

rejoicing

welcome

concept of triumph
of good over evil

4

LIGHTING CANDLES

Two candles are usually lit in a Jewish home on Friday evening to welcome Shabbat. This ceremony is most frequently performed by the woman of the household, who recites the blessing as she fans the light to spread the joy of the weekly festival.

Four candles are placed around an Advent wreath. They may be red or, as in the Roman Catholic tradition, three purple and one pink (for the third Sunday). One candle is lit for each of the four Sundays of Advent, a time of expectation and hope.

A fifth candle, a white one, may be added to the Advent wreath on Christmas day to celebrate the birth of Jesus, the light of the world in Christian thought.

Another single candle is blessed at Easter time. This Paschal candle will be a large one, perhaps with symbols of the death of Jesus and the letters alpha and omega, signifying the beginning and the end.

At a baptism in the Anglican community a small candle may be lit from the Paschal candle and handed to the parents of the child with these words: 'Receive this light. This is to show that you have passed from darkness into light; shine as the light of the world.'

A braided candle, often blue and white, is used for the Havdalah ceremony which ends Shabbat. The candle is held high, the original intention being to enable everyone to see its flame as a blessing was pronounced.

A crown of evergreens surmounted by several candles is worn by the Lucia queen in Swedish homes on December 13, on the day when they remember St. Lucia. In November there are the festivals of All Saints and All Souls, when the prayer says: 'Lighten our darkness........'

Put a white candle on top of an orange and you have a Christingle, a symbol designed by the Moravian community. The name means Christlight and a Christingle service is held in many churches at Christmas time.

Jewish families buy a box of forty four candles for the Hanukkah festival which lasts for eight days, with a daily increase in the number of candles used!

There is no limit to the number of divas, lighted wicks or nightlights, in these fire conscious days, for Diwali, the occasion on which Hindus honour the goddess Lakshmi, goddess of prosperity, and remember the Rama cycle of stories, while Sikhs think particularly about Guru Harogobind and the fight against oppression.

Just as an Indian family will put divas along the veranda, Roman Catholic families in Cologne put protected lights in the window on St. Ursula's day, October 21. It is a tradition there to honour the maiden, even though she lost her position in the Roman Catholic calendar reform of 1969. A procession goes around the streets by St. Ursula's church.

A memorial candle will be lit in a Jewish home during a period of mourning. The flame is a symbol of the soul as it goes heavenward.

A candle may represent a prayer. In some Christian churches candles are placed in front of the statue of Mary or one of the saints, as a Christian seeks help or gives thanks. All Saints day comes on November 1.

Candlemas is another candle day! On February 2 Christians remember that Mary and Joseph took their son to the temple in Jerusalem, where Simeon spoke about the child as a light (Luke 2. 25-33).

Whatever the festival, personal or community, the lights symbolise meaning, a welcome, hope and joy, a lift of the heart, anticipation or a dispelling of gloom. Explore these ideas as you light up!

FROM STORY TO CREATIVE WRITING

A stimulus

I sit and wait. The darkness is coming. The sun is setting beyond the window pane. Slowly the light fades and the gloom of dusk takes over. 'Let's light the candle.' A voice breaks the silence. 'Find the matches.' I listen as the matchbox rattles. A single stick is selected and struck against the side of the box. Its head bursts into flame, a bright flame that fills the room with a new yellow light, but a flame that quickly dies.

The stick is brought to where I stand, clean and upright in my own special holder. The flame touches my wick. I sizzle and slowly the centre of my being is lit. I begin to glow and my light spreads all round the room. I'm lifted up on to the highest shelf. My light shines, my light transforms the room. Normal activities can start again. My importance is taken for granted.

There I will stay until I've gone out, or until the time comes to put the room back into darkness.

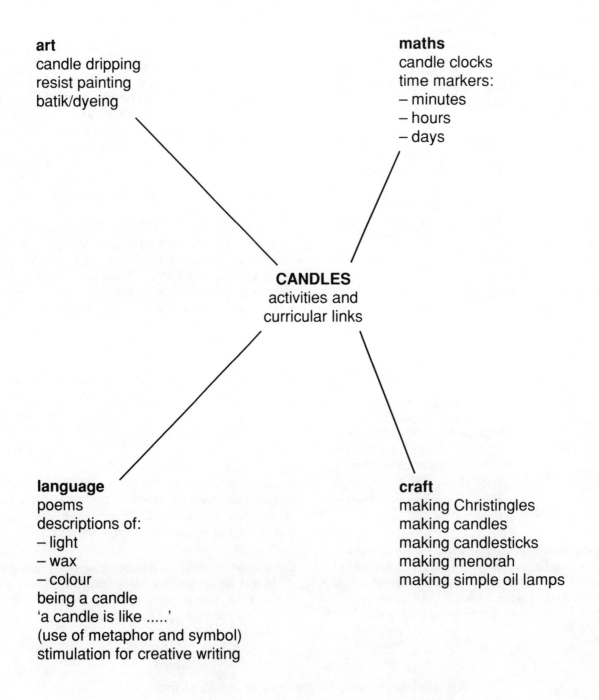

art
candle dripping
resist painting
batik/dyeing

maths
candle clocks
time markers:
– minutes
– hours
– days

CANDLES
activities and
curricular links

language
poems
descriptions of:
– light
– wax
– colour
being a candle
'a candle is like .....'
(use of metaphor and symbol)
stimulation for creative writing

craft
making Christingles
making candles
making candlesticks
making menorah
making simple oil lamps

HERE COMES A CANDLE

The children had been listening to the news headlines, a report of another bedroom fire in which a child had been badly burned. 'Mum, they said the boy had probably been lighting a candle,' said Jennifer. 'I wonder if it was his birthday?' Mum gave her attention to the newsreader as the full report was read. 'No!' she said. 'It was a power cut and the boy had been given a candle for a night light.' The children thought about the sad family, whose home had been damaged, and about the little boy in hospital. 'I thought candles were only for happy times,' said Paul.

'Make a list of the times when candles are lit, while I get your supper biscuits out,' suggested Mum, ' and I will tell you a story about a girl and a candle.' Jennifer rushed to find a ballpoint pen and paper. Paul started the list with *Birthdays*. Then Jennifer wrote *Hanukkah*. 'What's that?' said Paul. 'We learnt about it in school,' replied Jennifer. 'It is a Jewish festival when people remember a happy day. The Temple candlestick was relit after a war.' Paul thought of the next one. 'Put *nightlights* down to remember the little boy who was burned,' he suggested. 'Candles are often used for remembering,' said Mum, 'especially for remembering people who have died. Do you remember we saw a lady lighting a candle in Liverpool Cathedral after the Hillsborough disaster?'

The list grew longer as the children thought of other ideas and then Mum was ready with their supper and her story. 'These ought to be spicy biscuits,' she said, as she gave them rich tea fingers to eat with their blackcurrant drink, 'but I will explain that bit after I have told you the story.' And so she began.

'It was very dark as the girl crept out of the door, laden down with the baskets she held in each hand. Carefully she carried the precious supplies, just bread, cheese and fruit, but enough to keep her friends from starvation. As she came near the catacombs —' Paul interrupted. 'Mum, what are catacombs?' Mum thought for a moment. 'They were places where people were buried long ago. You might say they were underground passages with shelves cut into their sides, where people's bodies could rest. But in my story there were people hiding in the catacombs, Christians hiding from the emperor.' 'Get back to the girl, Mum,' pleaded Jennifer. 'Has she got a name?' 'Oh yes!' said Mum. 'Her name was Lucy or Lucia and the story says that, when she got to the catacombs, she put the baskets down while she lit the candle and fixed it on her head in a twisted ring of twigs. It was dark in the catacomb passages and she needed her hands for carrying the baskets. Every night Lucy came secretly to feed the hidden Christians and each night she lit a candle to help her find her way into the dark and mysterious catacombs.' Paul crunched the last bit of his biscuit. 'Why did you mention spicy biscuits?' he asked. 'Lucy lived over a thousand years ago but she is remembered on December 13, especially in Sweden because, in the dark winter days they liked the thought of that young girl carrying light and food into the darkness. So, every Swedish village has its Lucia queen for the day and one of the foods they eat is peperkakor, or spicy biscuits.' 'What about candles?' asked Jennifer sleepily. 'Oh, the Lucia queen wears a crown of evergreen twigs with candles stuck in it to bring light to every home she visits. So Swedish people remember Lucy's goodness.'

Jennifer and Paul started upstairs to bed. 'Here comes a candle to light you to bed, 'Jennifer muttered. 'Chip, chop, off with your head,' added Paul. 'That's what the emperor wanted to do to Lucy,' said Mum, 'and all because she used her candle to help hungry friends.'

RESOURCE MATERIALS FOR CANDLES

Those who have formed the habit of making their own poetry anthology have a valuable resource for the exploration of themes. Here is a starter list for our CANDLES idea.

A Birthday Poem by James Simmons comes in *All the Day Through* , edited by Wes Magee, 237 45597 9. Blowing out the candles as a bedtime ritual in the past is remembered in *Niddley, noddley,* illustrated by Jan Ormerod in *Rhymes Around the Day,* 14 050 424 9, and the necessity of the candle's light on a dark winter's day is recalled in *Bed in Summer* by Robert Louis Stevenson, *A Child's Garden of Verses,* 575 03727 X. *Light the Festive Candles,* Aileen Fisher, in *The Walker Book of Poetry,* 7445 0224 1, introduces the festival of Hanukkah which is outlined later in this pack.

Sayings and proverbs are also worth collecting. *It is better to light a candle than to curse the darkness* might prompt discussion amongst older juniors, leading to the writing of original stories which illustrate its idea. Shakespeare's Lorenzo in *The Merchant of Venice* says:

> How far that little candle throws his beams.
> So shines a good deed in a naughty world (V. i. 90).

Children may not get the point of *The game is not worth a candle* until they learn that the origin of the reference is to a poor effort, hardly worth the cost of the candle needed to light the players' card game.

Some children may remember the song they sang for St. Lucia's day, December 13, *Awake and light the candles bright;* an alternative version, *Now light one thousand Christmas lights,* is given in *Carol, Gaily Carol* 7136 1407 2. Other songs referring to candles are *Christmas candles* in Count Me In, 7136 2622 4 and *I have got a candle* in Jean Gilbert's *Festivals,* 19 321285 4.

Two junior story books may be found in the school library. *The Great Candle Scandal* is a rhymed story about the making of a paschal candle, written by Jean Chapman, 340 28116 2 and *The Christmas Candle,* 0719 7048 9, by Rod Broome is a story of reconciliation at Christmas. The story of a Greek girl who lights a candle for her sick grandmother is told in *We celebrate Easter,* a Bobby Kalman book, 86505 052 X.

Many infants want to concentrate on the birthday aspects of candles, so we shall make sure their book corner features *Kate's Party,* Joan Solomon, 241 89780 7, *Happy Birthday,* Satomi Ichikawa, 00 184860 7 and *My Visit to the Birthday Party,* 85210 719 7.

I am a Roman Catholic, 86313 258 8 and *I am a Greek Orthodox,* 86313 259 6 include references to the use of candles in Christian devotion and celebration. Look in the section on Hanukkah for references to the candles used in the Jewish festival.

Teachers who plan to introduce a candle-making activity may find useful information in *Festive Crafts,* Mary Anne Green, 584 11035 9. Those who want to introduce the symbolism of the Christingle candle will be helped by the leaflet issued by the Children's Society, Edward Rudolf House, Margery Street, London WC1 OJL.

GLORIOUS GLASS

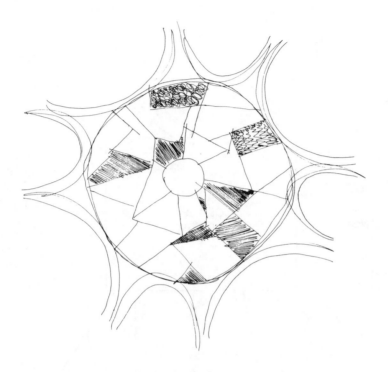

The inside of the building was gloomy and the child was bored. The sun came out and the scene changed dramatically. Blue, red and yellow patterns were spread across the floor and the child's expression reflected the brightness underfoot and the dust-laden rays of light from the window.

There may be occasions when a similar experience during a school visit will set the mood for a topic related to stained glass. Some children will be susceptible to the beauty of the colours and may comment on the way in which the effect of light on the glass enhances the atmosphere of the building. Some children will want to hear the stories described in the pictorial glass, while others may plan to carry out research on the symbols shown there. Some will be interested to try out the techniques and others may go away from the scene ready to reflect on the inner feelings evoked by the experience of light and shadow. In planning topics and in making reference to the teachers' objectives, related to knowledge, concepts, attitudes and skills, one acknowledges the variety of ways in which children respond at any given moment.

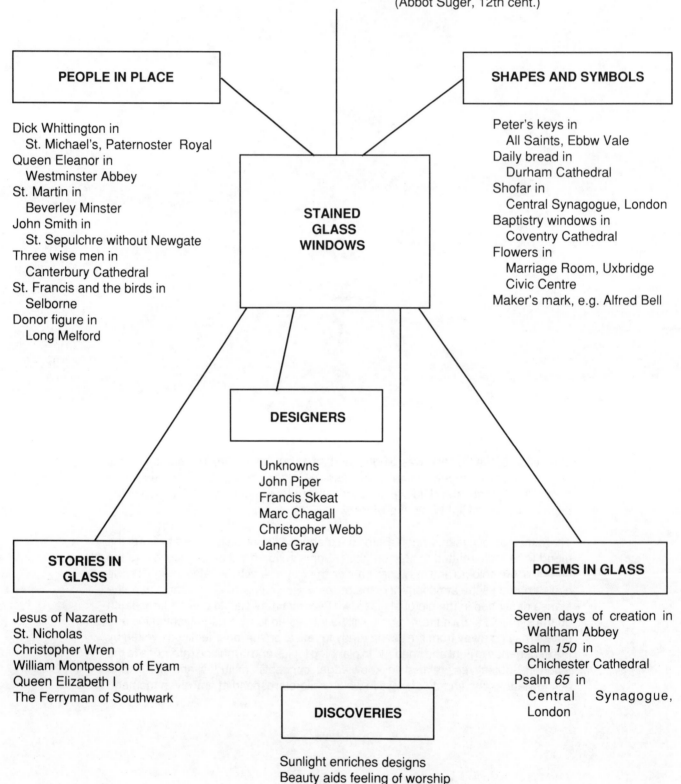

PURPOSE

Tell a story
Add to beauty of building
Interpret an idea
'To illumine men's minds so that they may
travel through it to an apprehension of God's light'
(Abbot Suger, 12th cent.)

PEOPLE IN PLACE

Dick Whittington in
    St. Michael's, Paternoster Royal
Queen Eleanor in
    Westminster Abbey
St. Martin in
    Beverley Minster
John Smith in
    St. Sepulchre without Newgate
Three wise men in
    Canterbury Cathedral
St. Francis and the birds in
    Selborne
Donor figure in
    Long Melford

SHAPES AND SYMBOLS

Peter's keys in
    All Saints, Ebbw Vale
Daily bread in
    Durham Cathedral
Shofar in
    Central Synagogue, London
Baptistry windows in
    Coventry Cathedral
Flowers in
    Marriage Room, Uxbridge
    Civic Centre
Maker's mark, e.g. Alfred Bell

**STAINED
GLASS
WINDOWS**

DESIGNERS

Unknowns
John Piper
Francis Skeat
Marc Chagall
Christopher Webb
Jane Gray

**STORIES IN
GLASS**

Jesus of Nazareth
St. Nicholas
Christopher Wren
William Montpesson of Eyam
Queen Elizabeth I
The Ferryman of Southwark

POEMS IN GLASS

Seven days of creation in
    Waltham Abbey
Psalm *150* in
    Chichester Cathedral
Psalm *65* in
    Central   Synagogue,
    London

DISCOVERIES

Sunlight enriches designs
Beauty aids feeling of worship
Windows may be memorials

PRIMARY TOPICS

GLASS TELLS A STORY

Once saints get into stained glass windows, their personalities become more perfect than real, and legends sparkle round their lives. So start the year with a recent saint, John Bosco, born in Italy in 1815 and noted for the practical help he gave to young apprentices and delinquents. His mother was roped into the job of housekeeper in the boarding house he opened for those learning the trades of the cobbler, tailor and printer in his workshops. His feast date is January 31. He is probably too recent to have a fixed emblem, so get the children to invent one.

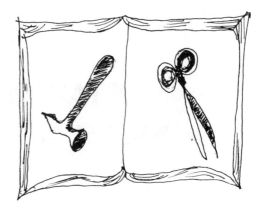

When colds and sore throats decimate our February classes, we might introduce the story of Blaise, said to have been put to death in the fourth century. A lady brought her son to him; a fish bone was stuck in the child's throat and he was dying. Blaise healed the boy and, later when he was in prison, the same lady brought him food and candles. So the feast of St. Blaise on February 3 is a time for blessing those with diseases of the throat; two candles are held in front of the sufferers.

April 3 is the day for Richard of Chichester, whose prayer has an appealing simplicity:

> May I know Thee more clearly,
> Love Thee more dearly,
> Follow Thee more nearly.

He needed all the saintly virtues, because King Henry III was violently opposed to his appointment as Bishop of Chichester. Given a home by another priest, Simon of Tarring, he persevered with his kindly work amongst the people of Sussex and eventually got access to the Bishop's palace.

One of the world's greatest modern artists was Marc Chagall. He was born in 1887 into a Jewish family in Russia. At the age of 63 he added stained glass to his approaches and used many memories from his early Jewish days as well as mixed images from the Torah and Bible. His images often link Jewish and Christian ideas. He once said: 'My art is a blue soul flooding over my paintings'. His work is found in many synagogues and community centres around the world. He died in 1985 at Saint-Paul in France.

September begins with a gentle hermit who cared for a wounded deer and ends with the reputedly irascible Jerome, who is usually portrayed with a lion. The story of Giles on September 1 is suitable for younger children; that of Jerome, the learned bible translator, is important in the history of religious writings and might be told to top juniors on September 30. Pictures of Jerome show him wearing a red cardinal's hat, another Christian emblem about which we talk.

For December we have two favourite children's saints. Nicholas of Myra is important for Dutch children on December 6 and St. Lucia's day is celebrated in Sweden on December 13. Perhaps we should concentrate on the modern celebration of her day but tell his story! He is patron saint of children, sailors and pawnbrokers, with three balls as his symbol. Hers is a platter on which her eyes are placed!

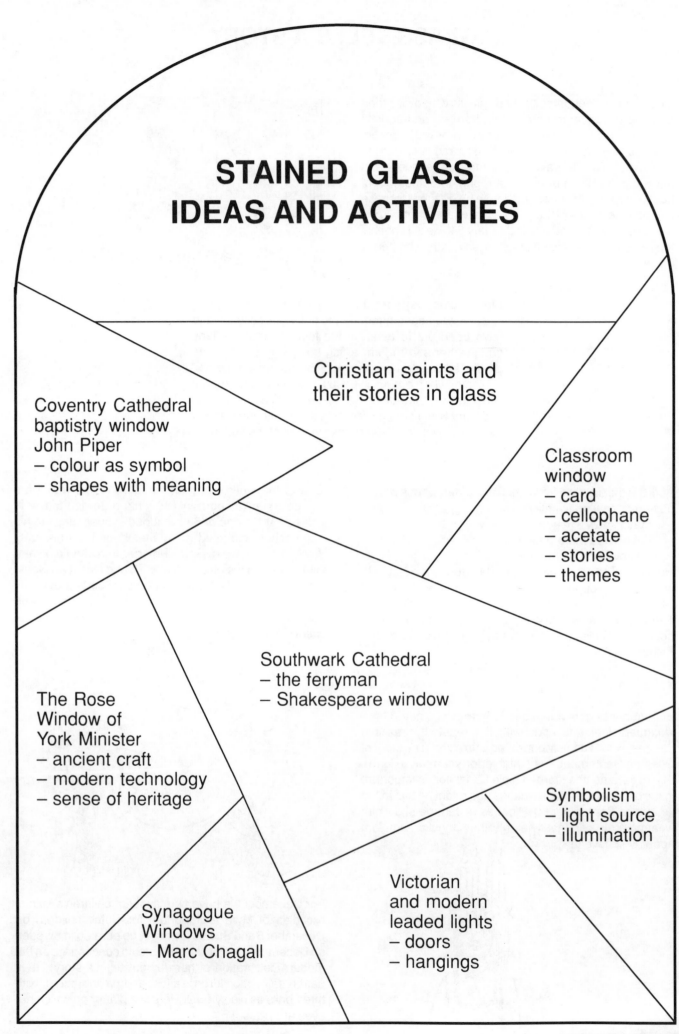

STAINED GLASS
IDEAS AND ACTIVITIES

Christian saints and
their stories in glass

Coventry Cathedral
baptistry window
John Piper
– colour as symbol
– shapes with meaning

Classroom
window
– card
– cellophane
– acetate
– stories
– themes

Southwark Cathedral
– the ferryman
– Shakespeare window

The Rose
Window of
York Minister
– ancient craft
– modern technology
– sense of heritage

Symbolism
– light source
– illumination

Synagogue
Windows
– Marc Chagall

Victorian
and modern
leaded lights
– doors
– hangings

THE LIGHT OF SAINT FRANCIS

'Gran said we ought to look at the stained glass window of St. Francis when we came to Selborne,' said Vicky and Neil. They stared up at the window. 'It doesn't look worth looking at,' muttered Neil. 'I can just see St. Francis in his brown habit and there are a few birds, but it is terribly dull.'

Just then the sun came out and everything looked different. 'Oh goodness!' said Vicky. 'Look at that little robin.' The children stared at the details of the window, birds, animals and flowers seemed so much better in the light of the sun. The little robin glowed in the bright light, his red breast sparkling. What a difference the light made to the window!

Back at school they told the class about the window showing St. Francis, and everyone decided that the saint would be a good person to use as their assembly topic. Soon everyone was doing research on Francis and before long they had made up three scenes about his life.

Vicky introduced the first scene. 'St. Francis is remembered for his care of animals and birds. One story tells how he met a boy on his way to market with a cage of doves. Francis paid for the doves and set them free.' Neil read the introduction to the second scene, while his friends made a tableau of the Christmas story. 'St. Francis is remembered in December when we put out our Christmas crib. He wanted the Christmas story to come alive for the villagers, so·he got real actors and animals to act out the scene in the stable.'

Ewan's turn came last. 'There is a prayer which Francis wrote. It includes these words:
    "Where there is hatred, let me sow love.
    Where there is darkness, let me bring light."

'One of the stories of St. Francis tells how he visited the district near Arrezo, only to find that the town was split in two by some quarrel. He sent his brother monk Silvester into the town to make peace. The monk sang songs of praise to God as he walked through the town gate and the people were so ashamed of their petty ways that they made up their quarrels.

'So Francis of Assisi is remembered as a saint, as one who cared about people and birds, and as one who brought light in a dark place.'

STAINED GLASS RESOURCES

A series of seasonal books from Wayland includes *Projects for Spring*, 85210 364 7, with a reference to the stained glass window in the Central Synagogue, London, and ideas for making a similar one.

Glass by Jane Chandler, 7136 2931 2, *Focus on Glass*, Graham Rickard, 85210 320 5 and *How it is Made: Glass*, Alan Peterson, 571 13411 4, are amongst the factual books which relate to our theme.

Stories of the saints seen in stained glass windows come in many forms, some of them more entertaining than indicative of the qualities which led to martyrdom and canonization. John Ryan's light style is evident in *A Bad Year for Dragons*, 370 31005 5. A powerful picture book on the same subject is *Saint George and the Dragon,* 19 279793 X. Teachers who want the sober facts and a survey of the legends are likely to refer to *The Oxford Dictionary of Saints,* David Farmer, 19 869120 3, or a similar book, many of which are on sale in Christian bookshops.

Where can we find interesting windows? Local contacts may give some help and some teachers may refer to *A Guide to Stained Glass in Britain,* Painton Cowen, 7181 2567 3, although it does not include synagogue or civic locations. Several religious bookshops, e.g. Mowbrays, and Southwark Cathedral sell plastic versions of stained glass figures and colouring sheets of window topics published by Hussingtree. *The Cathedral Stained Glass Colouring Book,* Ed Sibbett is published by Dover. Gift shops often have a selection of window plaques, showing flowers or birds painted on glass.

Our back cover is a window discovered in St. Andrew's and St. Mark's School in Surbiton. The window depicts the subject of 'the cross' and is a free interpretation of that theme, by a local glass artist, Tom Shapland, who died in the early 1970's. He designed other windows to be found in churches in Fulham, Battersea and Mottingham.

LIGHT

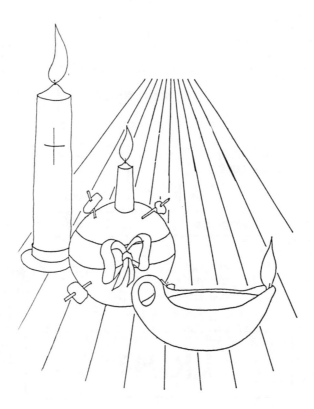

In one class a topic may prove to offer ideas for most of the term. In another situation, a similar topic may be a feature for a much shorter period. In one school a topic on light may be presented as an integrated opportunity. In another school, where work is structured more formally, the topic may be concentrated within one subject session, such as religious education. Two diagrams in this section suggest different ways of approaching the topic.

Sometimes the ethnic and faith composition of the class determines which religious features are stressed. The presence of one Jewish child in a church school class encouraged the teacher's introduction of the festival of Hanukkah, work supported by the eager contribution of that child's mother. Children of several faith backgrounds in another class enabled their teacher to draw on those various traditions, when basic work on aspects of light made understanding of the religious concepts associated with the theme possible.

A structured programme for the autumn term, November–December.

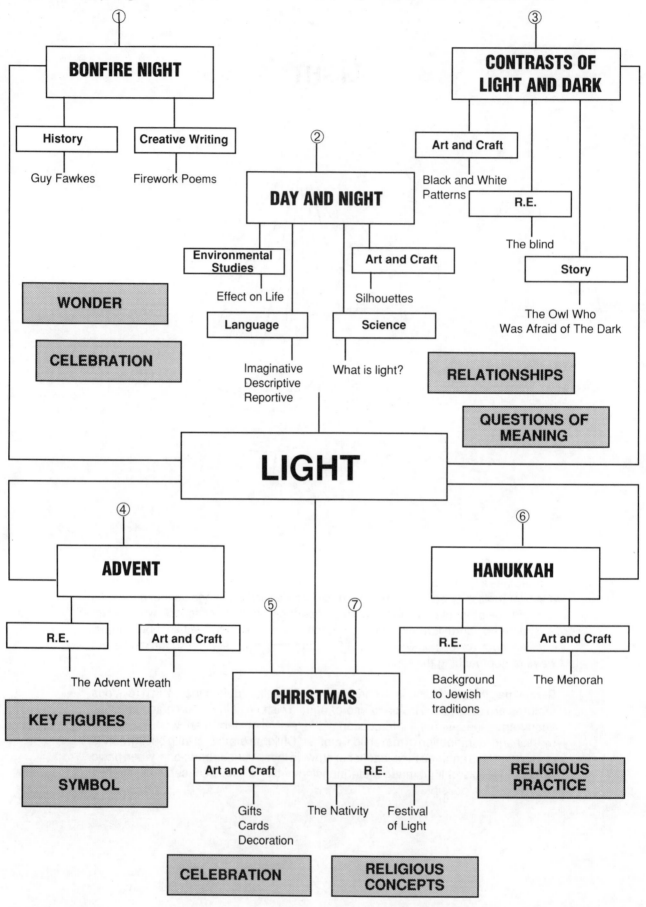

① BONFIRE NIGHT

History
Guy Fawkes

Creative Writing
Firework Poems

WONDER

CELEBRATION

② DAY AND NIGHT

Environmental Studies
Effect on Life

Language
Imaginative
Descriptive
Reportive

Art and Craft
Silhouettes

Science
What is light?

③ CONTRASTS OF LIGHT AND DARK

Art and Craft
Black and White Patterns

R.E.
The blind

Story
The Owl Who Was Afraid of The Dark

RELATIONSHIPS

QUESTIONS OF MEANING

LIGHT

④ ADVENT

R.E.

Art and Craft
The Advent Wreath

KEY FIGURES

SYMBOL

⑤ ⑦ CHRISTMAS

Art and Craft
Gifts
Cards
Decoration

R.E.
The Nativity   Festival of Light

CELEBRATION

RELIGIOUS CONCEPTS

⑥ HANUKKAH

R.E.
Background to Jewish traditions

Art and Craft
The Menorah

RELIGIOUS PRACTICE

An analysis of an integrated approach to the topic

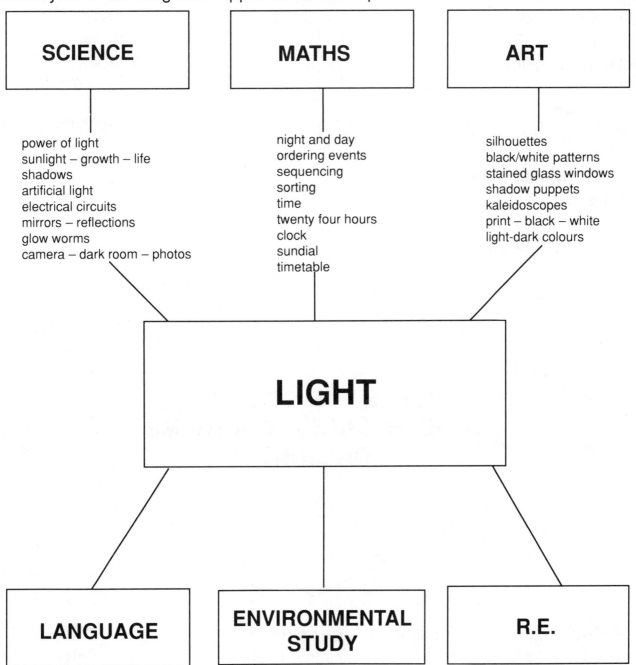

SCIENCE

power of light
sunlight – growth – life
shadows
artificial light
electrical circuits
mirrors – reflections
glow worms
camera – dark room – photos

MATHS

night and day
ordering events
sequencing
sorting
time
twenty four hours
clock
sundial
timetable

ART

silhouettes
black/white patterns
stained glass windows
shadow puppets
kaleidoscopes
print – black – white
light-dark colours

LIGHT

LANGUAGE

ENVIRONMENTAL STUDY

R.E.

experiences of
  excitement/surprise
  sorrow/comfort
  loneliness/support
  fear/trust
imaginative work on
  blindness
creative writing on
  fireworks
listening to story
  Good Night Owl
  The Lighthouse Keeper's
    Lunch
  The Owl who was Afraid
    of the Dark

different kinds – traffic lights
  of light   bicycle lamps
                  torch light
                  cats' eyes
                  candle
                  stars
                  lighthouse
                  beacon

nocturnal   – pets
activities   wild life
                 shift work

varied   – sun – warmth
messages   light in window – welcome
                 flashing light – warning

symbolism   – candles
                divas

festivals   – Diwali
                Hanukkah
                St. Lucia
                Christmas

light boxes
old shoe boxes

|

holes to let in light

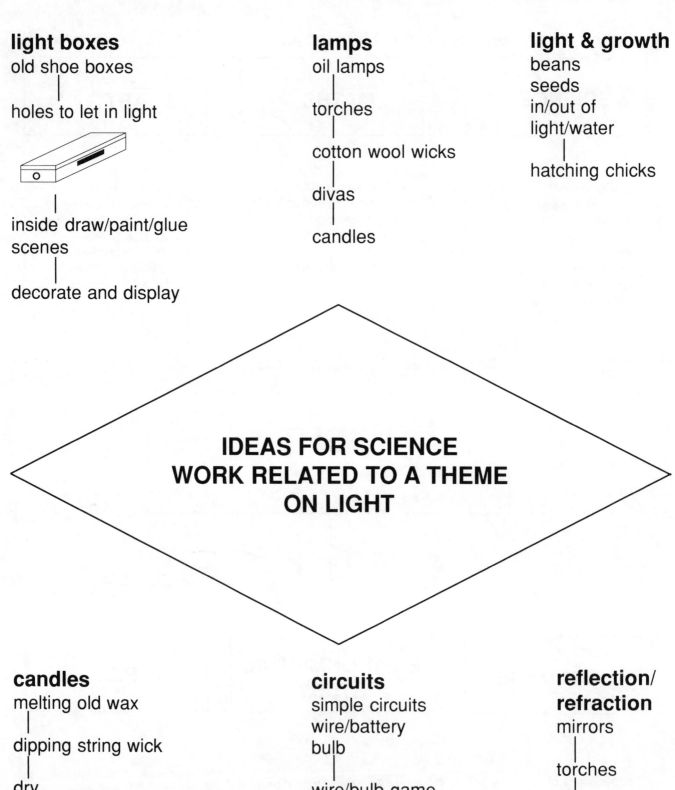

|

inside draw/paint/glue
scenes

|

decorate and display

lamps
oil lamps

|

torches

|

cotton wool wicks

|

divas

|

candles

light & growth
beans
seeds
in/out of
light/water

|

hatching chicks

IDEAS FOR SCIENCE
WORK RELATED TO A THEME
ON LIGHT

candles
melting old wax

|

dipping string wick

|

dry

|

more dipping

|

use/display

circuits
simple circuits
wire/battery
bulb

|

wire/bulb game

|

switches

reflection/
refraction
mirrors

|

torches

|

reflected
light

|

prisms

|

spectrum

|

kaleidoscopes

LIGHT FOR DIWALI

It looked as if Mr. Sharma and the children were getting on fine. The teacher peeped through the classroom window as she went towards the medical room with Peter, who had fallen in the playground. On a day when everything had gone wrong, it seemed a miracle that Mr. Sharma had arrived to give his promised talk about Diwali to her class and that he was quite happy to get started while she dealt with the emergency. 'Come on, Pete,' she said. 'Let's get cleaned up, so that both of us can find out what Mr. Sharma is telling the others.'

By the time they got to the classroom, the children were in small groups, talking and moving about with arms waving. 'Are you feeling all right now?' Mr. Sharma asked Pete. The boy nodded. 'Why don't you join Philip's group?' Mr. Sharma went on, glancing at the teacher for her approval. 'They are going to act part of the Rama story.'

Then Mr. Sharma turned to the teacher. 'Your suggestion of showing some objects was so helpful,' he said. 'I brought a statue of Rama, Sita and Hanuman and that kept everyone interested while I told part of the story. In fact, I only needed to start them off because the children seemed to know quite a lot already.'

The teacher looked towards the table where all the objects were displayed. 'Perhaps you could tell me about them while the children get on with their planning of the play,' she suggested. There was a book of rangoli patterns, a model of Lakshmi resting on a lotus flower, and some clay saucers. 'We devote one day of Diwali to the worship of Lakshmi, goddess of prosperity,' said Mr. Sharma. 'So families make beautiful patterns on their doorsteps, using rice flour, to attract Lakshmi to the house. The clay lamps are called divas and their light is another means of attracting the goddess.'

The teacher nodded and turned towards the bookshelf. 'We have collected some books to help us learn about Diwali,' she said, 'and the play you have organised will be very suitable for sharing with the whole school at Assembly.' Mr. Sharma clapped his hands and the children came back to the display table. 'Your acting had better be good,' he said to them. 'Everyone in the school is going to hear about Diwali and the happy return of Rama and Sita to their kingdom of Ayodhya. But now let's see who can tell Mrs. Elliot why Diwali is a festival of light — and it isn't just because we light divas!' The children wrinkled their foreheads as they thought. What answer would you have given?

RESOURCES ON LIGHT

There is no shortage of children's books about the scientific aspects of the topic. Some schools will have *Light and Dark,* 85078 526 X, in the Wayland *Science is Fun* series. Others will use Joy Richardson's book of the same title from Hodder, 340 42679 9. Those who have Macmillan materials may refer to the booklet *Light and Colour,* 333 28539 5, in the *Science Horizons* series; from Oxford *The Young Scientist Investigates* series has a topic book called *Light and Colour,* 19 918041 5.

Those who get interested in the mechanics of light in the modern world may enjoy *The Electrician,* an account of his work, for 6-9 year olds, 241 12573 1 or *Switch on a Light,* 241 12087 X.

Children who are fearful about the dark may be helped by stories like *Down in the Dark,* Helen East, 356 13513 6 and Susan Hill's *One Night at a Time,* 241 11229 X. *The Owl who was Afraid of the Dark,* Jill Tomlinson, is a favourite; teachers might like to try *One Moonlit Night,* Ronda and David Armitage, 14 050461 3. A new book in the ecology series by Hugh Lewin (remember *Jafta*) called *A Bamboo in the Wind,* 241 122147, deals with the plant's survival despite the flood which destroyed the community and speaks of the people's realisation that 'from the darkness we have come back to life,' as they rebuild alongside the bamboo groves. This might be used with stories of those who live in light although they cannot see it. Helen Keller is the obvious choice and a book about her, which teachers might use for reference, is published by Wayland, 85078 586 3.

Local Asian shops are likely to stock divas in the weeks running up to Diwali. Borough librarians in city districts often organise special events associated with the festival. Poster material from the Pictorial Charts Educational Trust, 27 Kirchen Road, Ealing, London W13 0UD is useful.

Maurice Lynch has prepared a booklet on *Diwali* which is available from the West London Institute R. E. Centre. Other agencies preparing material for teachers are the NW SHAP Primary Group, c/o Mrs. V. Barnett, 81 St. Mary's Road, Huyton, Merseyside, L36 5SR and the Minority Group Support Services, South Street, Hillfields, Coventry, CV1 5EJ. The CEM Mailing *Exploring a Theme: Festivals of Light* is another important resource.

THREE DAYS IN THE CHRISTIAN CALENDAR

Many teachers, parents, and those involved with children, have become increasingly concerned about the commercial trading in Hallowe'en. Whilst the media and the shops may provide a starting point related to the ancient origins of the festival, this topic targets the ways in which teachers may provide a different direction for the children's thinking. By exploring the lives of saints from every age, children may gain a deeper awareness of the concepts associated with Christian practice and with local custom.

The directions suggested here show how teachers can emphasise the positive aspects of this time of the year when Christians think about the relationship between All Hallows' Eve and the days of All Saints and All Souls.

THREE DAYS IN THE CHRISTIAN CALENDAR

All Hallows' Eve

October 31

Festival of Samhain,
Lord of Death

Warding off fear, death

Christian understanding,
Jesus overcame death

All Saints' Day

November 1

Remembering those who
served God, some 'officially'
recognised as saints and
all who have been 'Christ-like'

All Souls' Day

November 2

Pre-Reformation prayer for
souls in purgatory.

Remembering those who
have died.

concepts of good and evil	concept of courage	concept of sacrifice	concept of holiness	concept of commemoration

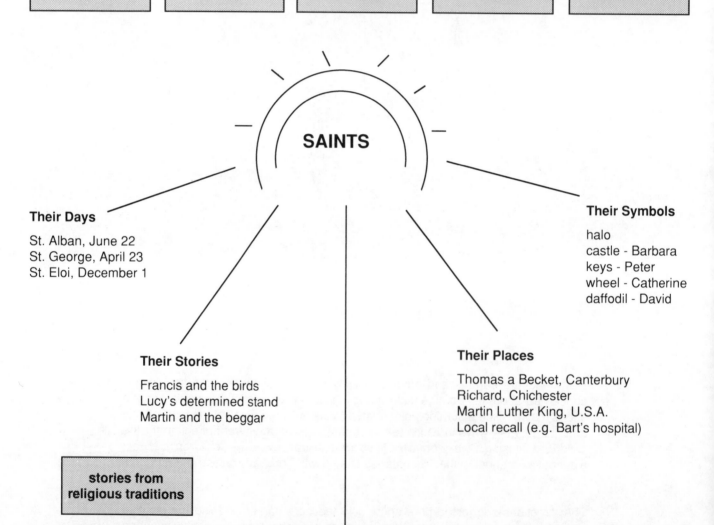

SAINTS

Their Days

St. Alban, June 22
St. George, April 23
St. Eloi, December 1

Their Symbols

halo
castle - Barbara
keys - Peter
wheel - Catherine
daffodil - David

Their Stories

Francis and the birds
Lucy's determined stand
Martin and the beggar

Their Places

Thomas a Becket, Canterbury
Richard, Chichester
Martin Luther King, U.S.A.
Local recall (e.g. Bart's hospital)

stories from religious traditions

Their Associations

Luke, patron saint of doctors
Nicholas, patron saint of children
Andrew, patron saint of Scotland
Cecilia, music
Teresa, prayer
Elizabeth Fry, prisoners
Gladys Aylward, children

religious practice

PRIMARY TOPICS

FILLING IN THE BACKGROUND

HALLOWE'EN (OCTOBER 31)

Hallowe'en is the popular name given to the evening before All Saints' Day (November 1). Its original name was All Hallows' Eve. It has its origins as far back as Celtic times in the Autumn/Winter festival of Samhain. Fire was an essential element in this ancient festival, hence the customs of bonfire lighting, candles and fireworks which are still used today. The Celtic festival was known to the Romans and incorporated into their festival to the fruit goddess Pomona. Elements of this are still seen in the apple-bobbing and nut-cracking games of modern Hallowe'en. The early church adapted all these festivals into All Hallows' Eve and it was widely thought that the souls of the dead re-visited their old homes at this time. The church tried to change the ancient celebration but never really succeeded; the Puritans did not allow it to be celebrated at all. It has become a less significant celebration in many churches and serious concern is felt about the connections with witchcraft and the occult in popular practice. This latter element is one which must be viewed with extreme caution if the season is introduced to children. Many customs that surround Hallowe'en are worth investigating, e.g. Tam O'Shanter by R. Burns, Lancashire's Teanday (Tean = Fire), Punky night in Somerset and Mischief night or Trick or Treat in the USA.

ALL SAINTS' DAY (NOVEMBER 1)

On this day all saints are remembered, despite the fact that many have their own special days. These are usually outstanding people who have lived particular lives of courage and faith. For many Christians this idea can extend to all who have been Christian. This festival is a day for giving thanks to God for their lives.

ALL SOULS' DAY (NOVEMBER 2)

This festival is often ignored in many parts of the church today, but was a day when all those who had died in the faith were prayed for. It had links with Celtic beliefs about the souls of the dead visiting earth to taste its food again.

All these occasions attempt to show the power of light over darkness and the victory of life over death. This prayer, The Third Collect for Aid against all Perils, sums up the feelings of this part of the year and is often said around this time :-

> Lighten our darkness, we beseech thee, O Lord;
> and by thy great mercy defend us from all perils
> and dangers of this night; for the love of thy
> only Son, Our Saviour, Jesus Christ. Amen.

Exploring Customs

Punky Night

Lancashire Tean Day

Trick or Treat (USA)

Make up your own ideas

Positive applications for
All Hallows' Eve

Exploring All Hallows'
by the Tower Church, London

Apple Bobbing

Pumpkin Pie

Looking at Saints

Stained Glass

Making windows of
a local saint e.g.
local parish, St. Nicholas or
St. Anne, etc.

Stories to re-tell

Special people for the
school or community

THREE DAYS IN THE
CHRISTIAN CALENDAR
ACTIVITIES AND IDEAS FOR
HALLOWE'EN, ALL SAINTS & ALL SOULS

Light and Dark

Prayers for the themes

Stories on the themes

Art work wax resist pictures

Fire pictures

Apples (close observation)

Pumpkins – drawn/cut and
painted (details observed)

Drama Work

Life of St. Francis

Life of St. Martin

Role Play — Empathy

Drama sequences

Links with local church or
school named after saint

Situations of fear & reassurance

MARTIN'S CLOAK

It was a bitterly cold winter's day. The soldiers were glad of their thick cloaks as they rode towards the town. 'It will be good to get into the city,' said one to his friend. 'We shall be protected from the fierce wind which blows across these open fields.' The other soldier nodded; his fingers were getting quite blue as he gripped the reins. It would be good to dismount and warm up by a fire and to hold a mug of hot soup.

Sure enough the town walls and the narrow streets made a big difference. The buildings seemed to shelter the soldiers from the worst of the wind and there was the added advantage of the warm welcome given by the people of Amiens. They stood at the side of the road and watched as the soldiers rode towards the city centre, led by Martin, their young captain.

Martin gazed at the crowds. There were the rich town leaders, warmly wrapped up in furs and fine wool. There were the children with mittens on their hands and scarves around their ears, protecting them from the cold as they jumped up and down in excitement. 'Give us a ride on your horse,' they yelled. There were the housewives with shawls over their heads. But there were also the down and outs. Martin caught sight of a poor beggar, sitting at the side of the road; he was shivering with cold. 'I must help him,' thought Martin and he felt in his pocket for some coins. But that pocket was empty — he had already given away that month's pay.

Martin shook his head. 'I must do something,' he thought. 'What can I do to help a beggar?' Quickly he dismounted from his horse as an idea occurred to him. He pulled off his thick army cloak and, with his sword, cut it in two. 'Here you are,' he said. 'This cloak is big enough for the two of us.' He wrapped one half around the beggar's thin shoulders, threw the second half round himself and rode forward with the rest of the soldiers.

That night Martin had a dream. He dreamt that he saw Jesus wearing the piece of cloak he had given to the beggar. Martin was still thinking about the meaning of this dream when the commander of the army sent for him. 'You have served the army well,' said the commander. 'I hope you will continue for a further period of service; we need men like you.' Martin shook his head. 'I joined the army to please my father. When the years of my service are completed, I want to fulfil my own ambition.' The commander was curious. 'Tell me about your plans,' he said. Martin explained. 'When I was a small boy, I met a follower of the Christian way. He thrilled me with the stories he told about Jesus. I resolved then to take up the sort of work done by Christians.' Martin paused for a moment and then went on; 'I joined the army at the insistence of my father — now I hope to obey the command of Jesus.' 'What is that?' asked his officer. 'The man I met so long ago told me that Jesus cared about the hungry, the ill, the stranger, the lonely, helping them in every possible way. When I saw that poor beggar in Amiens I remembered those stories. I think Jesus is commanding me to do what I can for the hungry, the cold and the poor,' answered Martin.

If you ever go to Trafalgar Square to feed the pigeons, look across to the famous church of St. Martin-in-the-Fields and remember the soldier who shared his cloak with a beggar.

RESOURCES FOR
THREE DAYS IN THE CHRISTIAN CALENDAR

A dash round the neighbourhood, looking at church notice boards, provides the names of some saints, whose stories could be researched by the children. If you are unlucky and the local church is called All Saints, suggest the children do their research on saints whose names are the same as pupils in the class. Surely you have a Martin, a Barbara, a Giles, an Andrew or a Lucy!

Whilst All Saints' day gives us a chance to talk about reasons why legendary elements come in many stories of those popular in medieval times, we shall turn to books like *Stories From The Christian World,* David Self, 356 11508 9, for twentieth century 'saints' like Dom Borelli and Mother Teresa.

Small medallions showing the figures of saints, and plastic or plaster statues, are available at Mowbrays, 28 Margaret St., London, W1N 7LB. Other stockists include Devotion, 52 Park Lane, Tottenham, N17, the Catholic Truth Society shop in the precinct leading to Westminster Cathedral, Victoria St., SW1, and Amen Greetings' Cards, 272 Mitcham Road, SW17 9NT. Postcards and icons showing Orthodox saints are sold at the St. Martin-in-the-Fields Bookshop, Trafalgar Square.

A new *celebrations* series from Wayland includes *Hallowe'en*, Hilary Lee-Corbin, 85 210 742 1, intended for the over-sevens. From the same publisher, with the same title, is the book for older pupils, written by Robin May, 85078 467 0.

Bobbie Kalman has edited a lively, but very American book called *We Celebrate Hallowe'en*, 86505 049 X. More serious in presentation and more cautious in its approach to the non-religious customs is *Hallowe'en, All Souls', and All Saints',* written by Anthony Ewens, 08 029280 1.

Those who are prepared to use stories about witches, cats and pumpkins as starting points for talking about feelings of fear and of the unknown, elements which may have led to the ancient customs, will have a collection of favourite titles. Some teachers will get out Meg and Mog, whose inventor Jan Pienkowski is so versatile. Some will have discovered Elizabeth Falconer's *Three Little Witches,* 1 85213 057 1, who go to school each morning to learn cooking, magic, spells and charms. *Witch Watch,* Paul Coltman, 233 98357 0, has a creepy feel about it, but reading it together might be a 'safe' way of dealing with children's fears at Hallowe'en. Mention witches and the children will immediately draw attention to *The Worst Witch,* Jill Murphy, 014 031108 4. Songs about witches and their broomsticks and a souling song are found in *Festivals,* Jean Gilbert, 19 321285 4. Another souling song is given in *A Musical Calendar of Festivals,* Barbara Cass-Beggs, 7062 4226 2, together with a Jack-o-lantern song. For this, and for other sections, it would be valuable to look through June Tillman's *Light The Candles,* 521 33969 3.

We cannot emphasise too strongly the need for teachers' discussion related to this season. In some areas, where children come from Christian or Muslim homes, parental feelings may be strongly expressed about any attempt to feature witches, even as a starting point. In the north of England, by contrast, the tradition of celebrating the lighter aspects of Hallowe'en is strong, and there may be no such difficulties.

HANUKKAH

The exploration of a particular festival will often provide the focal point for a topic, particularly with older junior children. It provides a valuable way of looking at a faith group, as well as enabling children to appreciate some of the deeper meanings experienced by the faith community at such a time.

The ideas suggested by the stories, food, games, cards and presents can be used alongside the symbols of light represented by the hanukkiah.

THE JEWISH COMMUNITY THINKS

about freedom from persecution
about the triumph of good over evil
about the courage of those who stand for the right
about liberty of worship
about the historical background of the festival
about God as Israel's deliverer
about loyalty to God and rejection of paganism
about the flame of faithfulness —

HANUKKAH

JEWISH CHILDREN ENJOY

the story of brave Judah
singing *Hanukkah is here*
a game with the dreidel
lighting the candles
packing of presents
making greetings' cards
potato latkes
receiving gelt

JEWISH FAMILIES HEAR STORIES

of the stand taken by Mattathias
of Hannah and her seven sons
of Judith and Holofernes
about the legend of the oil

THEIR ACTIVITIES INCLUDE

reciting the blessings
recalling deliverance from
enemies in many
historical events
singing *Maoz Tzur*
sharing a family party —

IN SCHOOLS MANY CHILDREN

hear about the festival
meet a rabbi at the synagogue

learn about customs through
which religious ideas are expressed

begin to understand the meaning of
the event to the Jewish community —

HANUKKAH

HISTORICAL BACKGROUND

The *Books of the Maccabees,* contained in the collection of writings described as the *Apocrypha,* and *Jewish Antiquities,* the history by Josephus, are sources for the story which stands behind the festival. Throughout their history, the kingdoms of Israel and Judea had been at the mercy of foreign powers, partly because of their strategic position in the Middle East. In the centuries following the conquests of Alexander the Great (356 - 323 BCE) the whole region underwent a process of hellenization, and Jews were amongst those involved in the adoption of Greek ways, although some opposed the process. For much of the period those Jews were able to follow their religious practices but, when Antiochus IV came to power in 175 B.C.E., he imposed more rigid regulations than did his predecessors. He forced Jews to bow down before Greek statues, ordered the death penalty for those who possessed a scroll of the Torah, desecrated the Temple, and murdered the elderly Eleazar who refused to eat pork. Ignoring Jewish belief in a hereditary priesthood, he nominated Menelaus as high priest, apparently in return for a financial consideration.

The inevitable uprising was led by a priest from Modin, Mattathias, and his five sons who formed a guerilla band operating from a mountain hideout. The sparking-off scene was the arrival of Antiochus' soldiers in Modin, coming to enforce the regulations. Although Mattathias proudly refused to obey, a fellow Jew valued his skin more than his faith and stepped forward to undertake the soldiers' command to sacrifice a pig. Mattathias pulled out his knife and killed the Jew who was ready to be a traitor to his people and their religion. In the skirmish which followed, the priest and his family escaped to the hills.

The guerillas were very successful in their attacks on the Syrian army and eventually managed to recapture Jerusalem, where an immediate task was the restoration of the Temple. Guards were posted on the city walls while the people hurried to respond to Judah's command. Exactly three years after its desecration, the Temple courtyards were filled with people gathered for celebration (164 B.C.E.). The festival of dedication, the first Hanukkah, did not end the war between Antiochus' forces and the Jewish guerillas. The death of Antiochus led to some diminution of the terrors and promises were made about freedom of worship, although the Syrians retained the right to appoint the high priest. It was not until 152 B.C.E., after the death of Judah, that his youngest brother became high priest and later, under another brother Simon, the Jews gained independence.

TRANSLITERATION

There are several variant spellings used in naming the festival and we need to remember that the initial H has a hard CH sound, as in Loch. Most common spellings are HANUKKAH, CHANUKAH, HANUKAH. It is sometimes suggested the eight-letter version is an appropriate reminder of the eight candles lit during the festival!

The Dreidel game

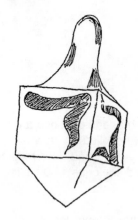

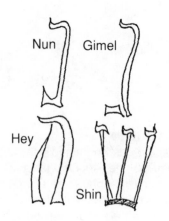

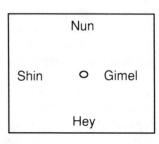

Cut out a square of card. Pierce a hole in the centre for a matchstick. Put the four letters at each side. (details on page 31)

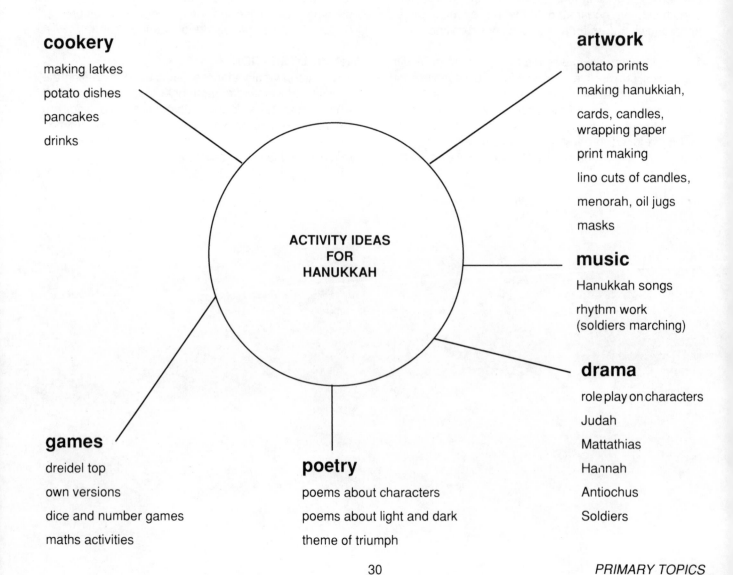

cookery

making latkes

potato dishes

pancakes

drinks

artwork

potato prints

making hanukkiah,

cards, candles, wrapping paper

print making

lino cuts of candles, menorah, oil jugs

masks

music

Hanukkah songs

rhythm work (soldiers marching)

ACTIVITY IDEAS FOR HANUKKAH

drama

role play on characters

Judah

Mattathias

Hannah

Antiochus

Soldiers

games

dreidel top

own versions

dice and number games

maths activities

poetry

poems about characters

poems about light and dark

theme of triumph

CUSTOMS OF HANUKKAH

THE DREIDEL
Games are part of Hanukkah fun. Some say that this relates to the pretend games which concealed the illegal study of Torah; a group of Jews would meet for reading and discussion of the law, posting a look-out so that, if soldiers approached, they could react to a warning signal, whip out a top and appear to be playing a game.

The dreidel is a spinning top decorated with four Hebrew letters, Nun, Gimel, Hey, Shin, now representing the phrase Nes Gadol Hayah Sham, Behold a great miracle happened there. Dreidel is a Yiddish word; sometimes the Hebrew, sevivon, may be used.

Each player has the same number of counters, nuts or sultanas and puts one in the middle. The first player spins the top. If it lands on Nun, the player does nothing; if it lands on Gimel he takes all the counters in the middle. When the top lands on Hey, the player takes half the counters but if it lands on Shin he has to add another to the pile. Before the second player has his turn everyone puts another counter on the pile.

FOOD
Potato and onion pancakes, called latkes (Yiddish) or levivot (Hebrew) make the special dish of the day for Jews of East European origin. Cooked in oil, they may be a reminder of the legend of the holy oil. In Israel it is customary to serve sufganiyot or doughnuts. One recipe for latkes reads like this:
> Finely grate an onion and six medium-sized potatoes. Leave to drain and then press out excess liquid. Mix with 1 oz. flour, salt, freshly ground black pepper and a beaten egg. Heat vegetable oil in pan and drop in spoonfuls of the coarse batter, flattening into round shape. Brown on both sides and serve hot.

Another range of Hanukkah food is associated with the story of Judith. Cheese dishes have been included on the Hanukkah menu since the fourteenth century, because it is said that Judith gave cheese to Holofernes, which made him so thirsty that he drank an excessive amount of wine, enabling her to overpower him while he was drunk.

For the children, parents may decide to provide biscuits cut out in festive shapes. It is possible to buy a set of cookie cutters with Jewish symbols, i.e. star of David, menorah, but families may like to design their own templates for a Hanukkah biscuit party.

HANUKKAH GELT
An old Jewish custom was to give children money or gelt at Hanukkah; this may be a reference to the time of Simon, the last Maccabee brother, who achieved political independence for his nation and so was able to mint a new coinage. Another suggestion is that this idea of giving coins began in Poland during the seventeenth century, not as a gift to the children but as a gift from them and their parents to their teachers. Tzedakah, helping those in need, is a Jewish practice and many families will have a tzedakah box in the home, so that coins collected during the Hanukkah period may be passed on to a chosen charity.

CARDS AND PRESENTS
Jewish families exchange cards and presents. In some homes children may receive mini-gifts on each of the eight nights! No doubt, children who have looked, in class, at shop examples of Hanukkah greetings' cards may want to devise their own cards to send to a Jewish friend. The obvious symbols to go on the cards are spinning tops, hanukkiot, jugs of oil, soldiers representing the two armies and the Temple of Jerusalem.

THE HANUKKIAH
Most Jewish homes have a special candelabrum for the festival; it has eight candleholders, plus a servant candle holder called a shamash, separated from the others. Wax candles are common but some Orthodox householders use oil lamps, since the Temple lamp was oil-filled. The eight lights are a reminder of the phial of holy oil which, in popular legend, lasted eight days at the rededication of the Temple in the time of Judah the Maccabee. Many designs are available on the hanukkiot; some show symbols of the twelve tribes, others portray tablets of the law, the lion of Judah or an oil jug.

On the first evening of Hanukkah one candle is put in the right hand holder and it is lit with the flame of the shamash candle. On the second night two candles are placed in position at that end of the hanukkiah and the left hand one is lit first, and so on. Some householders put their hanukkiah in the window after the candles have been lit and the blessings recited. These blessings include a reminder of the meaning of Hanukkah:
> We kindle these lights on account of the miracles, the deliverances and the wonders You performed for our fathers, by means of Your holy priests . . .

RESOURCE MATERIALS ON HANUKKAH

Information Books for Children

David Adler	*A Picture Book of Hanukkah*	8234 0574 8
Miriam Chaikin	*Light Another Candle*	89919 057 X
Douglas Charing	*The Jewish World*	356 07522 2
Susan Hughes	*We Celebrate Hanukkah*	86505 055 4
Clive Lawton	*I am a Jew*	86313 139 5
Judith Saypol	*My Very Own Chanukah*	9304 9403 2
Reuben Turner	*Jewish Festivals*	85078 558 8

Teachers' Reference

Naomi Black	*Celebration: the book of Jewish Festivals*	00 411602 X
Lynne Broadbent	*Hanukkah*	W. L. I. H. E.
Alan Brown	*Festivals of World Religions*	582 36196 6
Philip Goodman	*Hanukkah Anthology*	8267 0080 1
Mae Shafter Rockland	*The Hanukkah Book*	8052 0792 9
Lynne Scholefield	*Chanukah*	08 029276 3

Story Books

Leila Berg	*Hanukkah (in set of six titles)*	602 22688 0
Leo Pavlat	*Jewish Tales: The Eight Lights of the Hanukkiya*	856 13784 7
Isaac B. Singer	*The Power of Light*	8605 1258 4
Yehuda Wurtzal	*Lights*	940646 56 0

Songs and Poems

One Little Candle	*A Musical Calendar of Festivals*	7062 4226 2
Banish Darkness	*Festivals*	19 321285 4
Chanukah, Chanukah	*Festivals*	19 321285 4
Eight Little Candles	*Festivals*	19 321285 4
Light The Festival Candles	*Walker Book of Poetry*	7445 0224 1
Dreidel Song	*Walker Book of Read-along Rhymes*	7445 0770 7

Videos

Living Festivals — One	Pergamon Educational Productions
Lights	Scobus

Cassettes

Enjoy Chanukah At Home (Teachers' use, history, observances, music)	Eiber Productions
Latkes and Hamentaschen (16 Children's Songs)	Lemonstone

Artefacts

Hanukkiah, Candles, Dreidel, Gelt, Greetings Cards, Wrapping Paper, Israeli Commemorative Stamps.